Graduation With Civic Honors

Graduation With Civic Honors

◆

Unlock the Power of Community Opportunity

Nels Lindahl

iUniverse, Inc.

New York Lincoln Shanghai

Graduation With Civic Honors
Unlock the Power of Community Opportunity

iUniverse books may be ordered through booksellers or by contacting:

iUniverse
2021 Pine Lake Road, Suite 100
Lincoln, NE 68512
www.iuniverse.com
1-800-Authors (1-800-288-4677)

ISBN-13: 978-0-595-38979-7 (pbk)
ISBN-13: 978-0-595-83361-0 (ebk)
ISBN-10: 0-595-38979-1 (pbk)
ISBN-10: 0-595-83361-6 (ebk)

Printed in the United States of America

To Joni, Susan, Paul, Boyd, Jenifer, Gus Jr., Jason, Ben, Cheryl, Gus Sr., Joe, Bev, Twila, and John for support during the struggles of higher education.

Contents

The Story Behind Graduation
With Civic Honors

*Believing in a dream like graduation with civic honors is only the first step in
the process toward advocating the creation of a graduation with civic honors
program.*

The story behind graduation with civic honors began in an academic
setting during the spring semester of 2002 at the University of Kansas. I
took a class from Dr. H. George Frederickson entitled Concepts of Civil
Society. During the Concepts of Civil Society class, my collegiate interests
focused on civic engagement. At one point during the class, Dr. Frederickson posed a question to the class about what colleges could do to get people involved within the community. Over the course of the next year
thinking about the idea of civil society, I became interested in pursuing a
degree in the field of public administration. Thanks to the faculty of the
Public Administration Department at the University of Kansas, I decided
to endeavor to enter graduate school. I would like to thank Dr. Raymond
Davis for advice and guidance, Dr. Thomas Longoria for defining the
importance of collaboration, and Dr. H. George Frederickson for a
thoughtful introduction to the world of civil society.

Graduation with civic honors was only a dream until late in 2002. Dr.
Charles J. Carlsen, the president of Johnson County Community College,
learned of the idea from Susan Lindahl and, along with the board of trust-
ees and civic honors steering committee, envisioned becoming the first
community college in the state of Kansas to designate a graduation with
civic honors. In 2004, after Johnson County Community College developed the initial graduation with civic honors pilot program, the next step
was to start spreading the graduation with civic honors message. I was
honored to submit an article with Dr. Charles J. Carlsen and Susan
Lindahl entitled, "Civic Honors Program at Johnson County Community

College," to the *Journal for Civic Commitment* for publication. The resulting publication (Carlsen, Lindahl, & Lindahl, 2004) was the first step toward globally sharing the positive message of graduation with civic honors.

To realize the dream, students actually would have to graduate with civic honors. During the May 2005 graduation at Johnson County Community College, the dream became a reality when four students—including Deborah DeGrate, Carrie Donham, Chris Engle, and Jennifer Pittman-Leeper—were the first to graduate with civic honors. The story will be complete when students all over the world are graduating with civic honors.

1

What is Civic Engagement?

Society has experienced a true revival of public interest in civic engagement.
Robert Putnam's (2000) epic work *Bowling Alone* brought the idea of
civic participation to the forefront of the public mind. The value of civic
participation is essential to the process of value implementation in the
form of civic engagement. Civic engagement is a value choice, and the
implementation of that value choice is individual civic participation in the
community. One of the most basic definitions of civic engagement
involves thinking about how government, society, and citizens interact. In
terms of how scholars discuss civic engagement, the definition takes on a
benevolent feel, referencing citizen activities that benefit civil society.
Strengthening civic engagement, in practice, involves building civic skills,
increasing active voter participation, and using public service announce-
ments to encourage volunteering to strengthen civil society. Watershed
events like 9-11 have created a reflective sense of national interest and significantly increased the willingness of individuals to participate in civic
engagement.

The best way to describe civic engagement is to take a step back from
current views and look from the perspective of the potential benefits that
higher civic engagement provides society. Civic engagement is increasing
civic participation by encouraging participation in civil society. That participation could come in the form of volunteering, campaigning, or even
discussing community issues with neighbors. Increasing civic participation
through civic engagement breaks down the disconnect between individuals and the community. Robert Putnam (2000) clearly made the case that
individuals within modern society largely have replaced community activities with social isolation. Helping to break down the disconnect between

the individual and the community is valuable to strengthening the community. Reciprocally, strengthening the community through civic engagement increases the amount of active participation within the community.

How does one spread the ethic of civic engagement? Civic engagement has to come from fostering strong community leadership from both professionals and community organization leaders. These leaders give the community a significant advantage by creating a long-term vision for increasing civic engagement. Civic participation through active civic engagement can involve spreading the ethic of volunteerism. Allowing individuals to work for community organizations is an important part of growing the capacity and size of civic engagement within the community.

Defining civic engagement in terms of communities involves identifying three different types of communities. We have communities of place, idea, and circumstance. Individuals can participate in issues associated with the place where they live as a form of civic participation based on engaging in core issues that determine the structure of the community. Neighborhood groups have the potential to facilitate civic engagement by offering a venue for civic participation in the community. Civic engagement also can be fostered by communities of ideas where individuals within the community can come together to participate in dialogue and action about specific issues. Civic engagement surrounding communities of circumstance often focuses on volunteering and resolving community-oriented problems.

Now is the time to move forward to increase civic engagement within civil society. Civic engagement is a most important emerging value because of its potential to strengthen the social fabric and the community as a whole. Programs like graduation with civic honors can encourage practical solutions to increasing civic engagement like emphasizing the necessity of recognizing a commitment to civic engagement. Graduation with civic honors is a way to institutionalize the encouragement of civic engagement through official and public recognition. Society should recognize that academic achievement and civic engagement go hand in hand. For higher education to benefit society, educators cannot merely educate people. Educators must strive to educate people to become good citizens.

Building a good society fosters a community that encourages collaboration and engagement from every citizen within society.

Higher education is the key to moving forward as a society. We have to be able to educate future generations about the importance of civic engagement. Being able to inform future generations of the potential benefits of increasing civic engagement through encouraging volunteering and civic participation is essential to building a stronger society. Civic engagement truly is the ability of an individual to be a vibrant part of the community by participating in the betterment of society. However, devising practical ideas that can encourage civic engagement is more difficult than it sounds. That is why high-reward, low-cost solutions like graduation with civic honors can bring civic engagement to the forefront of higher education.

Currently, the Civic Honors Project lobbies to spread the word about graduation with civic honors and strives to work and collaborate with organizations that have an impact on the community. The current graduation with civic honors initiative focuses on identifying potential avenues for expanding the number of higher education institutions offering graduation with civic honors.

2

What is Civic Honors?

The idea of civic honors is for the community to be able to acknowledge those individuals who are active participants within the community.

The current design of the graduation with civic honors program requires implementation by a university to bridge academics and involvement in community. The implementation of this idea involves connecting education to society, first at the university level, then at the national level by replication of the program. A positive underlying message of the graduation with civic honors program is the possibility to spread change within the community. Graduation with civic honors can become a part of the very fabric of the community. The program is inherently sounding the call for individuals to play a larger role in fulfilling the needs of the community by finding not only organizations that they feel benefit the community, but also organizations with which program members want to work. The program begins with the college providing the opportunity for individuals to volunteer within the community and by providing an accurate list and descriptions of opportunities that will allow these individuals to find opportunities that resonate with them.

Graduation with civic honors provides a platform for a message about the opportunities to work with the community. The first step is speaking to individuals, organizations, and universities that have the potential to develop vibrant graduation with civic honors programs. The message is about what is possible within the community and how to use technology to bring people together. A graduation with civic honors program strives to create a positive message about the potential of community. Replication is imperative for success. Graduation with civic honors can be more than a program at one university in one community; it should expand to society in general.

It is critical to be aware that resistance to change may occur as a response to changes to traditional ways individuals become involved in the community. This is critical during the early development of the program (Osborne & Gaebler, 1992) but may continue to be an issue. A goal of the program is to work within the community without regard for politics but for the benefit of the society, drawing out the civility or the virtue of citizens to enhance society (Rouner, 2000). The program allows citizens to develop a strong sense of community while empowering them with the belief that action is possible. The process creates a model of proactive behavior that enhances volunteering within the community (Bell, 1999).

The graduation with civic honors concept relies on the university as a principle source for implementing and designing the civic honors program. It is possible for any college to implement and design the program. This does not mean that universities are the only organizations within the community that can be the instruments for change to develop their own civic honors programs. Therefore, during the formative period, the discussion at a university also could be a model for organizations in local and regional networks. The positive nature of the message that the civic honors programs can spread does not exclude any actor or organizations from participation. Collaboration and inclusion is the basic assumption that will enable community building in any community and develop a stronger society as a whole. The discussion of civic society in America does not rely on the assumption that civil society is inherent to democratization. Organizations within the community are capable of broadening the concept of civil society in a way that really can benefit the community (Stanton, 1999).

3

Thinking About What is Possible

When working to strengthen the community, anything is possible, and any time alternatives are not considered, potential is lost.

Imagine a world where everyone who wanted to volunteer some of their time had one place they could go to find out how to participate. Understanding what is possible requires recognizing that individuals are all different and that bringing together all of their individual strengths, capacity, and skill specializations will benefit the community (Gulick & Urwick, 1937). Imagine, if you will, a world where no gap exists between the individual who wants to benefit society and the organizations that desperately need additional help from volunteers. Imagine a world full of accessible information provided by universities and other organizations engaged in graduation with civic honors. This is possible with the right amount of time and effort. It is an idea that quickly can become reality with the right motivation and intentions. It is possible to motivate individuals by focusing on individual civic attitudes and participation within the community (Barber, 1984). It is also very important to start designing the graduation with civic honors program with this end in mind. One of the first steps is to identify how the program can realize the vision of what is possible (Covey, 1989).

This vision of what is possible includes all of the individuals within the community. All of these individuals can gain from realization of the vision of the university. This vision should allow the community to organize in a way that capitalizes upon both what is possible and what already exists within the community. The vision involves recognizing and leveraging the strengths of individuals to serve the needs of the community. Thinking about what is possible for the individual within a given community is essential to connecting the worlds of possibility and potential accomplishment. Some skepticism exists about whether or not it is possible to change civil society by developing programs to respond to practical problems within society (Dionne, 1998). The questions result from the assumption that strengthening civil society is such a noble idea that programs do not receive an appropriate level of scrutiny. Any reservations about the graduation with civic honors program should and will receive attention within the following pages.

What occurs within this vision is a program that, over time, recruits a body of individuals to participate within the community. It is important to identify an extensive pool of individuals within the university. Many individuals have the potential to make a difference in the community. The university can bridge with organizations within the community to create seamless access for individuals interested in volunteering. Moreover, this program creates a powerful dynamic between the community's needs and the university, which fits the mission of most universities. Within the current civil society, this power dynamic already may exist within some organizations. To create an environment conducive to change, the entire community does not have to be willing to participate in the civic honors program, but the entire community should know that the program exists. It may take some bold and strong organizations that are willing to start graduation with civic honors programs to get the ball rolling. Each person graduating with civic honors has the potential to be a community leader who can provide not only vision but also long-term stewardship of the ideas behind the introduction of a civic honors program.

This charge is important to the community overall because it opens the door for not only leadership but also realistic change within the community. Many students are already volunteering in the community, perhaps through a service learning program on campus or as part of a church, synagogue, or club initiative. The civic honors program relies on a partnership to get people involved and to allow organizations to communicate their needs to the community. The charge specifically is to foster the development of community by making it easier for individuals to participate within the community, while creating visible recognition at graduation for those who worked for the community as well as for themselves. This simple idea is the backbone of mobilizing thinking of the community as a network of individuals with infinite potential that can strengthen the community. A university can become a strategic partner with the community, willing to facilitate communication between individuals and organizations from the perspective that anything is possible.

Transforming the vision of a civic honors program into a reality involves a considerable amount of leadership and innovation. The university may view the creation of a civic honors program also from the perspective that it is a bridge to enhance connection between the university and the community by enabling individual action to strengthen the community. Understanding what is possible through the civic honors program involves being able to see the new levels of potential broader community impact. A graduation with civic honors program endeavors to unlock a world of potential that transcends the walls of the university and strengthens the social fabric of the community.

4

Vision and Universities

Being able to see what is possible is the key to knowing what has to be achieved within the community.

Why is this community vision important to the university? It provides the opportunity to start something with the potential to expand beyond the boundaries of the university and to have a lasting positive effect on the surrounding community and students. The graduation with civic honors concept provides a chance for some institutions to become national leaders by creating a vision and by providing a model for socially beneficial civic engagement. Engaging the program as a way for the university to unite the community behind the mobilization of individuals is an avenue toward community success. Becoming a vibrant partner with the community through such a program raises the perceived level of commitment on the part of the college. Vision is a necessary component of being a leader in the community. Change is inevitable. Without being prepared to address community issues and changes, the university will miss opportunities. It is important to focus on being able to anticipate changes in society and to deal with that change in a positive way (Johnson, 1998).

The legacy of the program can be a profoundly important page in the history of the university. It has the potential to make the college or university an active part of the community as a real part of its daily life, and that legacy would pay dividends to the college. Results include providing a positive message for the university to spread to its current and prospective students, showing that academics can go hand in hand with the strength of the community. Fostering the development of strong community around the university also is essential to a healthy university environment. The long-term potential of each college or university program is to expand beyond the institution by serving as a model for other institutions and, as importantly, to spread the positive image of the institution.

A college or university that has particular success with the civic honors program could become a national model that not only would spread a message of community, but also would build recognition of the college as a national leader. This also creates the potential to identify strong leaders within the institution by providing opportunity to those who work hard toward building a strong community. These leaders have the potential to build the reputation of the institution as well as the community. This potential for vision and leadership requires nurturing. It is the foundation of building a working model for developing a strong community. The success a university has with the civic honors program is more than success for the university; it is also success in the greater context of what the volunteers contribute to the community. Defining action in the context of community is the first step to being able to understand what actions will produce positive results within the community.

Why is this concept so powerful for the community? It shows that the university has the vision to be a social leader in the community. Those creating a graduation with civic honors program must think about not only building the social fabric that holds the community together but also enabling current potential in the community. The fact that an institution within the community is stepping forward to assume a position of leadership is a powerful message to the community. It validates that leadership is possible and that community stakeholders can make a difference. This dynamic of power in the community is very interesting to think about in that spreading a positive message about community can have an impact on the community itself. Looking at leadership and ways to benefit the community is a powerful use of vision that can have profound effects.

Would it be beneficial to the university to unite the community within the spirit of collaboration? Any way that the spirit of collaboration can spread within a community sends an important message about uniting the community. Implementing a program that spreads a message about collaboration within the community can serve as a rallying cry. Positive uses of the language of community emerge that will help define the context of the entire endeavor. One of the cornerstones of ensuring that collaboration is possible is being able to develop a civic honors program that benefits everyone involved. When all the parties involved benefit in some way, the community as a whole benefits from greater sustainability.

IS THE CIVIC HONORS PROGRAM FEASIBLE?

Being able to look beyond what is possible and to understand what is feasible takes not only perspective but also a drive to move in new directions.

The resources and technology exist to create the program, and the university has the leadership ability to make this program a reality. The university already has the internal organization necessary to track students. This foundation of information makes implementation of the internal civic honors program much simpler than the implementation of the external program. The internal program only has to deal with students and coordinate declaring the civic honors within the university. The external program is more complex, as it requires working with outside organizations to develop a database that is accessible not only to these organizations but also to members of the community. The basis for long-term development of the civic honors program within the community is being able to work with individuals outside the university.

A civic honors program is unlikely to develop spontaneously within the community without the backing of a strong organization like a college or university. The institution has the resource of its students to connect or bridge to the community. The development of a rich and complex civil society will not just appear. It has to be a part of the vision of an institution willing to acknowledge that advanced industrialization and technology alone will not create a sustainable and efficient program for developing the community (Fukuyama, 1995). To develop a strong civic honors program, the institution has to acknowledge the difference between developing a strategy for constructing a stronger civil society and just developing technology for the sake of developing technology. The institution has to design the civic honors program based on utilizing the strengths of developing technology to benefit society. One of the benefits of advancing technology is lowering the cost to implement a civic honors program.

The civic honors program is free to outside organizations, providing a true resource for the community. Leadership rarely takes the form of something that organizations within the community can use without having to commit fiscal resources. This is fundamental to opening the door to organizations, K–12 schools, and colleges and universities to adopt the civic honors program. No organization in the community is likely to turn down the opportunity to utilize this resource. Open and free access builds the possibility of mobilizing organizations toward wanting to participate in the civic honors program. The ability to develop the interest of both the individual and the organization is important to sustained success of the program in the community.

Volunteers are exactly what the community organizations need: a labor pool that is accessible and does not require funding to recruit. The outside organizations in the civic honors program only need to announce and maintain a current list of activities, with some description of the activity and time requirements and the number of people they would like to participate in each activity. This ability to have the need identified for potential participants is where the real power of the civic honors program originates: the ability to develop that relationship between the individual and the community organizations. The organizations do not have to pay for television commercials or newspaper ads to recruit these individuals. That frees up other resources for the organizations and allows them to participate in the civic honors program without having to commit their resources.

If the model works, the civic honors program starts to spread throughout the community, the region, and the nation, developing into full-fledged community action. A national program showing the promise of the program on a broad basis could help to build success. Community involvement is rarely an unpopular issue. This program involves a truly altruistic purpose; the only real obstacle is if the community organizations perceive the civic honors program as competing with them in some way. However, this perception is unlikely, as the only competition that develops from a civic honors program is for volunteers. The program itself is not inherently a competitive system; it is a system of pure collaboration, connecting people who will work to those who need help, working together for the common good.

Selling the first partners will be the biggest hurdle. Once it is apparent that the program is successful, collaboration should become easier every time an organization becomes involved. The momentum should build as organizations start seeing the tangible benefits of the civic honors program. Organizations will be willing to participate in a program that works. The first hurdle will be fostering early participation in the program by outside organizations. Ironically, at inception the civic honors program may appear ineffective, since many outside organizations will not know about the program, resulting in a limited list of organizations and activities for which to volunteer. It will take great vision and commitment to develop the foundation necessary for the civic honors program to be successful. The demand for participation of volunteers exists in most communities; thus, it is likely that the potential volunteers themselves will have outside organizations in mind already. This has been the case in the Johnson County Community College program.

A program design that is nonpolitical on the issue of helping the community also should help to manage opposition. It is very important that the civic honors program appear not to be competing for political power but to be working to foster social capital—not for the good of the institution running the civic honors program but for the general good. The program should work with the community to develop the natural strengths in the community. That dynamic is inherently a nonpolitical community issue in which every member of the community could and should be a stakeholder. There is a question of whether everybody can come together to work for the common good without being drawn into use as a political campaign tool. The civic honors program needs to be a step away from partisanship—an effort to increase civic participation.

It should not be difficult to obtain a foundation grant to design a community organization activities database and to set it up as a model for other institutions. In today's world, the database design allows organizations to post information to the Web. This will require thought and planning, because the database needs to be capable of handling multiple situations and of serving as the model for future programs. Specifically, the initial database design should allow another institution to install and use it to start a civic honors program. If the database design does not allow collaboration, the initial investment to design the database would be a burden to every organization trying to set up a civic honors program. Again, obtaining funding to design a national model for the civic honors database would simplify the matter.

The cost to design this database is not extreme. Most institutions are already using databases and have individuals on the payroll who specialize in designing and implementing such databases. This puts the institution in a unique position to utilize current resources with some application of time and leadership to develop a broad community partnership. An institution that has the leadership to design a repeatable database is imperative to the rapid spread of the civic honors program throughout the nation. The foundation of the civic honors program is a message worth repeating, that advocating increased civic participation is beneficial to society. An institution could take credit for origination of the database, to build its reputation.

5

Thinking About Civic Honors

A civic honors movement is more than just a program; it is a set of ideas about benefiting the community.

Universities have the power to motivate social change in the community by engaging the public in civic participation. Having a long-term perspective regarding the benefits of increasing civic participation is fundamental to implementing the vision. The university must take a step back and focus on the "community" part of its contract with the community. The community's partnerships with government will rise and fall over time; the university can provide stewardship with respect to civic society within the community. It is participating as a cornerstone of civic action, a place to mobilize the population and to introduce people to the world of community service. An initial benefit is fostering a sense of community by offering recognition for achievement in community service through a graduation with civic honors program.

The civic honors program is not just a way to reward students, but also a model to bring the community together, rallying around the university. In this model, the university becomes not just brick and mortar but a living part of the community. Every action within the civic honors program relies on the concept that every series of actions must benefit the community. Being able to focus the actions within the community toward the purpose of benefiting society will help develop an effective distribution of authority (Merton, 1957). A civic honors program has the capacity to empower volunteers, the university, and the community to strengthen civic participation through better focused and more widespread active participation. That active participation design links individuals to the community with opportunities that did not exist before creating a stronger civic community (Skocpol & Fiorina, 1999).

By the university becoming a centralized location, many organizations in the community can acknowledge their need for volunteers. Organizations become empowered to have a voice in the community via a central location to make the connection between people willing to participate and the organizations with a need. This centralization becomes a powerful tool to address the disconnect between individuals and the community. The power of a strong civic honors program comes from organizations in the community understanding that the university is a natural part of the community. This enables identifying needs and facilitating the direction of willing participants to fill these needs. In the end, this provides a stable source of information for the community.

The university would be able to keep this information in a central place that is viewable by anyone at any time. Being able to coordinate the needs of the community amplifies the voice of individual organizations and identifies the demand or need. Building a database of organizations within the community that need volunteers is a powerful way to identify the gaps in participation. The power of this situation exists in the ability to identify the needs of the community and to serve as an information exchange for students as well as members of the community. Students who are motivated and interested in volunteering in the community will be able to find a connection with an organization that needs assistance. The university will be able to track the trends and patterns within the community itself, providing a valuable statistical view.

Thinking about organizations participating in the civic honors program requires understanding of the relationship between informal and formal organizations. The civic honors program needs to formalize communication between organizations, transforming informal organizational linkages into formal ones. Transparent evaluation of the program will avoid creating confusion within the community, allowing the unified message of civic honors to expand behind the support of formal organizations (Barnard, 1938). Connecting volunteers with information develops in two ways. First, it strengthens the bond between the community and the student by facilitating participation in the form of civic engagement. Second, it allows the university to develop a connection within the community by providing a service that pays dividends to the community and also introduces individuals to the rewards of civic engagement. The student volunteers participating in the program are recognized and rewarded through presentation of the title "Civic Honors." They receive a tangible recognition of their service to the community, and the program strengthens the bond between the citizen, community, and college. Graduation with civic honors pairs academics and the community in the eyes of the audience. Using the powerful association of the idea, the university is not only an institution of higher education, but also a partner with the community.

To conclude, the civic honors program concept has the capacity to empower volunteers with the opportunity of civic engagement. The university becomes a central part of strengthening the community through active participation. Participation occurs through the art of expanding communication between the individual and the organization. An essential step is the understanding that communication is essential to being effective and successful (Alinsky, 1971). Collaboration is the key to the future of the civic honors program concept. As soon as one university is willing to start the program and to provide a database of those organizations needing assistance, nothing will stop other universities from using this structure to facilitate volunteering in the community. Building the database for the civic honors program is the cornerstone of creating the ability to expand the program. Information management will determine the long-term viability of the civic honors program. The long-term success of the civic honors program can motivate social change in the community by engaging the public in civic participation, benefiting society as a whole. For an organization initially formed by community advocates to survive, it has to start looking for places to expand and ways to find external support (Downs, 1966).

CIVIC HONORS: SHORT-TERM IMPLEMENTATION

Designing a realistic civic honors program that can be quickly implemented will take diligent hard work and planning.

In the beginning, it will be important to create a program that can expand and that has its foundation in the community. This will require planning for the long term as well as looking at strategic issues. Without making a conscious effort to look at the issues of implementation, the final product probably will not produce the intended results. This will require using scientific management to look at these issues and a focus on using statistics to help check the overall efficiency and effectiveness of the civic honors program (Taylor, 1911). It is also important to spread a clear message effectively and efficiently. The message and the program must spread throughout other communities. Without focusing on the repetition of the message, program implementation may occur without the program surviving as a model to facilitate future collaboration. Without the potential for future collaboration, the civic honors program cannot be self-sustaining with respect to spreading as a national model.

It is also important to think about the personnel who will be implementing the civic honors program. The administrators of the program will have to carry the flag of collaboration; thinking in terms of policy execution is inherently important (Goodnow, 1967). Building a strong team of individuals who have the knowledge and experience to carry out the civic honors program is only one part of designing the team. Also important is being able either to motivate those individuals to be advocates for the civic honors program or to find individuals who already believe in the ideals of strengthening the community and will be self-motivated to become advocates of the civic honors message. The individuals involved in implementing the program and technology have to be motivated and driven.

Building a database that is efficient in delivering the desired information as well as effective in allowing communication is critical to success. Having a database that can be mobile and spread to other universities will help enable a prototype for others to follow. The database must allow students to find opportunities within the community in which to volunteer and must allow the organizations listing those opportunities to update their information. Developing tools to help organizations to update their information quickly and efficiently is integral in the development of a successful civic honors program. Centralizing accurate information is a distinct part of setting up a system with a seamless exchange of information. The need for the transfer of information between organizations and individuals is an important dynamic. Program planners should design an administrative system for the civic honors program that allows complex interactions between individuals and organizations with the smallest amount of resistance from red tape as well (Simon, 1947).

Designing a successful database will dictate the number of people needed to manage the program implementation and monitor the database. If the database is interactive with both the individual and the organization, constant updating by the university will be unnecessary. Designing the database to work with the internal university civic honors program will make the system easier to operate, track, and maintain. Of course, the database will need monitoring by an administrator to make sure that the organizations are keeping their information up to date and that the requests for volunteers are legitimate. These kinds of questions are what make thinking about the design of the database so important to the success of any civic honors program. Without having the preliminary planning time to think about these difficult issues, the program could require significant amounts of technical support from the university. A database set up in a way that allows posting from organizations will become self-sustaining. A feature will also need to remove filled positions from the database. This will make it possible to move the majority of maintenance work to the organizations themselves, making the posting service dynamic.

The database is not the only part of the civic honors program that needs careful planning in the beginning. Having a strategy to get the message out about the program to the community is also a very important part of design and implementation. Making use of local media and newspapers is essential to spreading the message to the community. However, the message presented to the students of the university is also important. The introduction of the program to the university is a very important part of the implementation strategy. Planners may think about the implementation in terms of developing an initial beta test of the database with only part of the university, with a strategy to expand the program as it builds momentum.

The need for expandability of the civic honors program also requires thinking about the scalability of the program design. The posting system should be Web based, which would require bandwidth and a computer running the database. This is where the experience of the university's technology department becomes an exceptional resource. Since most of the background information and personnel already exist within the structure of the university, the design and implementation can ensure the success of the civic honors program. The management of this process will require leadership and vision from the university team that develops the model but will become easier as the network of university civic honors programs develops. It is also important to think about the individuals who will be developing and representing that network. The individuals involved in the street-level administration of the program will administer the program daily and thus will define how the program really works (Lipsky, 1980).

Developing a system for students to accept volunteering opportunities that is traceable is essential to providing the quantitative evidence to support civic involvement benefits. Moreover, it is an essential part of a successful civic honors program, because this system provides the information necessary to understand program implementation. Allowing the university to see the actual numbers of participants in real time allows analysis and reporting of the development of the program that will benefit students and community. Such ongoing analysis will help identify areas that need the most work and help identify strengths within the program. Long-term trends in the community also can be analyzed. The power of having accurate information about the development of the program allows the university to guide its own direction and to understand what is necessary to measure changes in the community.

Having the perspective to develop the system so that it requires almost no staff and maintenance to keep costs under control is essential to making the program as beneficial to the university as possible. Thinking about how to control costs and information during the development and implementation of the program will pay dividends. If the civic honors program becomes a substantial drain on time and technology from the university, the initial design did not maximize efficiency and economy. One of the most efficient opportunities in the creation of a civic honors program is the ability to delegate the program to a current university division with existing resources.

Setting a target date for the program long in advance allows the development of a program that can expand at a certain rate. It allows the program to take shape around an implementation date, which helps focus the direction of the program and gives it credibility as a concrete implementation, rather than a theoretical plan. Organizations within the community can think about how they are going to interact with the program and can develop strategies to become involved. The viability of the civic honors program hinges on the ability of the university to involve organizations in the program during development so that the database is not empty when the implementation date arrives.

Really developing a comprehensive plan to implement the program is going to be difficult for the first university to build a model. After the first model is established, the playbook for developing the program will only need to be refined for each university. Of course, understanding the individual environment of the civic honors program community will have an impact on implementation and adaptation over time (Thompson, 1967). Designing a program by applying analytical techniques to the design process will yield a better program overall (Mintzberg, 1979). The civic honors system design should instill a strong ethical sense in those individuals participating in as well as administering the civic honors program. Administrators have the responsibility of controlling the organizational arrangements to prevent unethical activities (Meier, 1979). The potential loss of ethics would damage the positive nature of the message of civic honors about getting individuals involved within the community.

CIVIC HONORS: EXPANDING WITH ORGANIZATIONS

Organizations have the capacity to build the civic honors network through existing community networks.

The civic honors program, once implemented, can expand without boundaries. One of the best ways to expand the civic honors program is by thinking in terms of organizations. At implementation, the university will need to identify key groups of organizations within specific categories. Allowing organizations within those categories to spread the message about the civic honors program will ensure its success. Using existing networks within the community to expand the civic honors program is a definite goal to enhance success. Existing networks will allow organizations to work with each other and to discuss being a part of the civic honors network. The civic honors program cannot remain static; things will change, and policies and administrations will shift. However, with a good strategy for expansion, change will be positive (Bozeman & Straussman, 1990).

CIVIC HONORS: LONG-TERM MAINTENANCE

Stewardship is not just a function of leadership; it is a necessary part of building a civic honors program that will benefit the community.

The maintenance of the program will require a significant amount of planning when the program is started. The stewardship of the program will require that the university be an advocate for the spread of the civic honors model. Therefore, the university must develop a model in a clear and concise fashion. This is where the long-term stewardship of initial civic honors programs will help the development of other civic honors programs. Once the groundwork has been established, expansion of the program into a national network of community action will become increasingly easy.

Defining the message in ways the media can report is very important to selling the message. Managing public promotion of the program is essential to the program's political survival and growth (Rourke, 1984). From time to time material needs to be made available to the media that can be condensed to a sound bite or a series of statistics that can sell the message. Using public statements to deliver the civic honors message will help shape the community's perception of the civic honors program (Blumethal, 1979). The university has to become an advocate of the civic honors program in the community. Organizations need the ability to think in terms of creating a comprehensive strategy for getting the message out in the long term. This means developing a strategy where accomplishments of the program are communicated to the media and thinking of ways to manage the image of the program at the community level. If the program is not continually part of public discussion, it could lose momentum, and involvement will suffer. Thus, the media strategy is very important to the success of the civic honors program over time. Public information regarding the program must resonate with the community.

Having the long-term perspective that measurable statistics will be important to the long-term success of the program is lacking in today's programming at most colleges. Statistics will become very necessary in evaluating the success of the civic honors program within both the university and the community. Some kind of process has to keep statistics up to date; a committee could identify the long-term trends in organizational posting and in volunteering. This is essential to measuring the development of the program. Evaluation also will require a critical discussion of the implementation strategy as a whole. Feedback will enable the civic honors program to correct for changes in the environment of the community and also to identify parts of the program that are not working correctly (Katz & Kahn, 1966). Identifying trends and ideas that will benefit the civic honors program will develop a better civic honors program. Individuals also will feel that their message is being heard. To prevent individual disenfranchisement when people have comments and suggestions about the potential of the civic honors program, it is important to provide a platform where their comments are part of the discussion.

Identifying the need for stewardship of the civic honors program with respect to the growth of the program and the new directions it could take will require leadership within the university. Such leadership not only will set up a review system to evaluate the program internally, but also will develop mechanisms to recruit new partners. To recruit new partners the university will have to become an advocate for selling the idea and looking at the program from the perspective of expansion. Without thinking in terms of how to expand the program, the potential for spreading the message about the civic honors program is lost.

THE COSTS TO THE UNIVERSITY

If the civic honors program is designed to be cost effective, it has the greatest potential for long-term benefit to society.

For the most part the civic honors program should be relatively inexpensive; the university already should have the technology to implement the database and the ability to add responsibly to certain divisions. What will be complex is creating a system for stewardship of the program and perhaps having a program administrator. Implementing the civic honors program as a whole will require the time commitment of staff members and the reputation of the university. The university must allocate resources to design and implement the database and must set up a strategy for system maintenance. Establishing the program in a current division of the university will provide a beta site for its implementation. Any successful program for the university will need to focus on having the utmost possible efficiency and the lowest possible costs of time and money (Wilson, 1889).

The civic honors program in action will determine most of the cost with respect to attention to detail and efficiency. For the most part, the implementation of the civic honors program will drive the cost. Since the design of that implementation is by the university, the opportunity to control costs is on a university-to-university basis. Universities have to be attentive to issues of the state budget and the expectation that good fiscal times will come and go, so the civic honors program requires efficiency and economy.

6

How Civic Honors Benefit Society

Any time it is possible to achieve something that can truly benefit society, it should be pursued to its full potential.

Understanding changes in just a few aspects of society sets the foundation for looking at the bigger picture of potential benefits to society as a whole (Putnam, 2000). The bigger picture includes the foundations of not only community, but also the individuals within the community. That said, an empowered population is a powerful population. That power extends well beyond the sphere of influence of each individual and fosters the collective sense of being a community. This very distinction should be rewarded enough to view action as possible and to use a positive frame of mind when considering the possibility of mobilizing a collective effort to address the community's problems.

It is important not only to look at specific conditions where the civic honors program benefits society as a whole, but also to break down some of these instances to understand what exactly the program does for society. This involves looking at the complex relationships between individuals in the community and the establishment of some general trends emerging from a successful civic honors program. It is hard to argue that the mobilization of people within society for the common good is a bad proposition. However, it is important not to rush to judgment on the issue and to take the time to think about the implications for society as a whole. This requires being able to take a step back and look critically at the interactions that occur within communities and think about the assumptions behind them. One of the most basic assumptions about civic honors is that working to strengthen society is a step in the right direction for forging a just society. Taking the first step requires believing that a society where individuals work to benefit the community is a decent society. Working toward the end of developing a decent society is a necessary step in benefiting the community as a whole (Margalit, 1996).

INCREASING CIVIC PARTICIPATION

The best way to benefit the community as a whole is to get more individuals involved in the spirit of civic participation.

One of the ultimate goals of the civic honors program is to increase civic participation by mobilizing the people of the community in the interest of building a spirit of volunteerism, which results in strengthening participation. When individuals feel enfranchised by being able to gain something tangible from the civic honors program, a positive feeling is generated, not only from working with the community, but also generalized to the community at large. The hope is that this feeling of goodwill will take the form of a feeling of ownership in the community and a heightened general interest in the outcomes of the community. This should extend not only to the community service, but also to the broader context of civic participation. In this context, specifically, community service becomes the means to address a problem much broader than just being a part of the community. The result is an individual's feeling a sense of community by being empowered to view action as possible in the greater context.

It is important to take a step back and view the civic honors program at this level to allow for a broader discussion of community as a whole. In context, something is often missing in programs that focus on very specific sets of problems. Understanding the greater impact on the population is an important part of being able to guide a program in the right direction. Working toward the goal of increasing civic participation in the community is the critical first step in being able to allow individuals to work within the community. When individuals are helping to increase civic participation with their action, they feel like they are truly making a difference. This distinction of individual action as not only part of the greater good as a whole, but also a conscious effort for the betterment of society sends a powerful message. This message will resonate with the individual who is already working in the community and will show other individuals that action is possible and makes a difference.

The higher the level of civic participation in the community, the better off society will be in general. Devoting time and energy to the programs that most desperately need assistance removes strain on government to address these problems and also allows the time of the organization to be better spent on helping the community rather than having to recruit volunteers. This has the added benefit of allowing organizations to become more ambitious in working with complex problems by having the power of community mobilization supporting their efforts. Graduation with civic honors can help fill the gaps between what is possible and what currently happens due to, in most cases, a lack of volunteers to accomplish the mission of the organization. A major part of connecting individuals is using communication technologies. Graduation with civic honors is an idea that can engage the community by utilizing emerging technologies to enhance communication.

BREAKING DOWN A DISCONNECT BETWEEN INDIVIDUALS AND THE COMMUNITY

Bringing the community together through building connections between individuals and the community is the basis of strengthening the social fabric.

One of the most important parts of any action within the community is to identify the stakeholders involved and the problems they have in common. The biggest problem facing both the individual and the organization is not motivation or finance; it is the connection between the two. Understanding that individuals and members of the organization may not understand this connection is key to addressing not only the disconnect but also the challenge of managing the flow of information.

In a perfect world, the flow of information would be seamless. Anyone who wanted to participate in the community would know where every opportunity was and who needed the most assistance. A primary goal is to focus the direction of the civic honors program on making connections between individuals and organizations. This is accomplished first and foremost by informing the individual of the opportunity to participate and then facilitating the connection between the individual and the organization by managing the information about organizations' needs. A first step toward solving the problem of this disconnect would be establishing a central place in the community that would allow development of seamless information between individuals in the community labor pool and the organizations within the community that need assistance.

This would benefit society and the community by allowing individuals who are seeking to participate within the community a way to find out how to participate. Removing the miscommunication between organizations and individuals also enables the individual to find organizations whose goals the individual feels are worthwhile. The benefit of this relationship is that individuals will be motivated more to work toward a cause that they believe in than just to fill the needs of an organization. Individuals can be selective in how they find community service opportunities, which empowers them to work in a way that they feel is most appropriate. Having a centralized system of record keeping and communication drastically reduces the time and effort involved, which would be overwhelming for the individual.

Becoming more efficient in connecting individuals and organizations will save time and allow more time to be spent actually volunteering. It also will alleviate some of the problem of the disenfranchisement of individuals who feel they cannot find a suitable place to volunteer. Finally, this efficient connection will alleviate the problems associated with individuals' not being aware that the problems exist in the first place, if categories and opportunities are not clear.

STRENGTHENING THE COMMUNITY

Bringing together the community is the only way truly to build strength within the community.

Any time people can be brought together in a way that adds strength to the community in general, society is bettered as a whole. Being able to address the problems within each community is a feasible way to influence society as a whole. Thus, the civic honors program could change the face of society by allowing change to occur in every community. This is possible by strengthening each community by building the network of volunteers and allowing change to occur on the street level. Allowing organizations to address very real problems in a very grass roots way further allows the community to identify its needs and then to have the strength to allocate resources to those organizations. Without thinking about the rewards of individual and group responsibility, it will not be possible to see the existing potential to strengthen civil society (Wolfe, 1989).

The key foundation of how a community builds strength is not having to rewrite everything that is currently positive, but allowing the strengths of the community to overcome existing difficulties. Thus, the civic honors program can work to develop the pool of individuals willing to participate and can allow the natural leadership of the community to bridge the gaps in the current system. The idea of focusing on the natural abilities of individuals and organizations is the basis of a powerful positive message, strengthening what is at the very heart of the community.

Fostering the strength of the community has to be the foundation of any successful program to implement social change. This requires thinking not just about individuals and organizations, but also about the long-term benefits of their actions. In the end, organizations can focus on what problems need to be solved. Creating a positive environment of hope is essential to getting people involved in the community as a whole. If each individual's action can be associated with strengthening the community, as a whole that message of individual action will pay dividends in involvement in the community. People need to be involved and positive about the community to build strength that will translate into social capital. It is important to understand that using the potential of every local circumstance is important to taking advantage of the potential of strengthening the community (Putnam, 2002).

Foundations of civic renewal within the community occur through the message that each individual can contribute. In the long term, this will be one of the most beneficial parts of any program that provides opportunities for each person to make a difference. It also has the compounding effect of making it easier to make a difference with each person who gets involved. The grass roots effect of spreading the word through personal efficacy and personal victory is one of the most powerful and empowering experiences that can strengthen the community.

INCREASING THE AMOUNT OF ACTIVE PARTICIPATION

Having individuals involved in the community benefits society, but having active participation has the potential for long-term benefit.

Every single time one person gets involved in the civic honors program, the potential increases to spread that message. If that potential can be nurtured and sustained, that individual remains involved from the positive rewards of being part of the community and is also able to create personal connections. Allowing the participants to help recruit from the community has the potential to increase active participation. It is important to reward those who are willing to participate with the recognition of civic honors and to acknowledge the effect of fostering an ethic of volunteerism. Developing that ethic and sustaining it with opportunity and reward is not only important to active participation in the long term, but also raises the awareness of the community.

One of the most powerful parts of any civic honors program is the ability to track the amount of involvement and the needs of organizations over time. Such tracking provides an accurate measure of participation. Being able to measure the rate of participation and to chart the increases in participation helps manage the level of participation. Evaluating the level of active participation helps the community address concerns about the level of participation. Over the long run, if participation decreases, the community can use tracking data to identify which organizations need the most help and to issue a call for specific assistance. Being able to see the trends of active participants will require understanding what organizations are doing to empower the individual and will allow other programs to look at success as a model.

This will set the foundation of a sustainable model of learning about what it takes to get people involved and to keep them involved. Having the perspective to be concerned about the long-term stewardship of the civic honors program will pay dividends in active participation. Being able to view in real time the needs of the community not only will help foundations allocate money and city officials understand the depths of the problems, but even more importantly will call attention to possible problems before they become serious issues for the community. Allowing the community to be proactive with respect to addressing issues in real time will be powerful beyond measure to benefit society.

STRONG LEADERSHIP IN THE COMMUNITY

The potential exists within every community; it takes strong leadership to unlock that potential.

Every organization will have stronger leadership when the issue is transformed from how do we get people involved to how do we get things done. This transformation will introduce new individuals to the organization who have the potential to lead and serve to expand the learning curve on leadership. Each time the organization interacts with the individual, learning occurs. It is significant that learning on the organization level allows the potential for learning from the community level. When the leaders of the community have the information necessary to make good decisions, the potential for leadership in the community grows every day. That potential for growth in the community is provided by strong leadership and is essential to the long-term success of a community. Being able to identify those leaders is vital, because the program's message can be amplified with strong leadership.

When an organization steps forward, fosters the development of a civic honors program, and extends that program to the community, it creates a strong voice within the community. The organization becomes a steward of the community spirit and is there to lead within the community. The development of community leaders is essential, and the flow of information to them about what is actually going on will allow them to lead with a vision. That ability for long-term leadership will benefit society as a whole and will allow the community to work most effectively.

The ability of leaders to focus on what is occurring within society will add a level of perspective to facilitate long-term planning and the development necessary for change to occur. When the community is strong, the job of a successful leader becomes one of sustaining that strength and translating it to ways to benefit society.

THE ADVANTAGE OF HAVING LONG-TERM VISION

Being able to see what is possible within the community and having the courage to move in that direction are what vision is all about.

Sometimes it is necessary to be able to see what will happen in the long term or at least to plan for possible outcomes. This type of perspective is necessary to see what could happen with programs like civic honors and other community organizations that have the ability to influence the future of the community. Overall, it is important think about the development of community through the participation of the individuals within the community. Thinking of ways to engage the individual and to help organize the organizations is the foundation of strengthening the community. This engagement and organization presents several advantages for the community by allowing infrastructure to keep up with demand and also by facilitating the flow of capital.

Keeping track of what going on is as important as what is going on within the community. Tracking is critical to success; lacking the presence of mind to evaluate what is happening can result in missing some opportunities. The community has to be vigilant at identifying opportunities as well as at looking at current challenges. The challenges of the future will be difficult to address if there is no system to evaluate each developing challenge, much less to anticipate and be proactive about such challenges. One of the great values added to the community is the ability to shift resources from problems that have resolution to problems that are developing or need to be addressed.

SPREADING THE ETHIC OF VOLUNTEERISM

It is one thing to benefit the community. However, to benefit individuals with a lifelong gift of volunteering is priceless.

The power of any civic honors program is to mobilize the individual to participate within the community. One of the goals of the civic honors program is to spread the ethic of volunteerism to the individual for life. Being able to get college-age students to participate in community and to develop the ethic of volunteerism early in life sustains growth in the community. A sustainable strategy for developing an ethic of volunteerism can be a cornerstone of successful maintenance. Being able to maintain a strong civic honors program is the foundation of building a strong community; in a sense the two are strongly related. Pursuing the building blocks of a strong community is a solid strategy for sustaining not only community development, but also an ethic of volunteerism.

Being able to sustain an ethic of volunteerism within the community is a key factor in the success of any community program. Sustaining that ethic requires a lot of planning and long-term vision. Identifying issues that could cause individual disenfranchisement can help reduce the possibility that individuals willing to participate lose hope. It also helps ensure that those individuals who have developed a strong ethic of volunteerism will not lose hope. Focusing on possibilities for expanding volunteerism includes spreading a positive message about what is possible within the community. Providing a vision of what is possible is a way to unify individuals who care about the community with one powerful message. Unifying the community with a strong consistent message will foster an ethic of volunteerism. The individual with that ethic wants to believe that the system is working and beneficial.

Long-term solutions for disseminating a positive message within the community require planning and the stewardship of strong community leaders in partnership. Without stewardship of the message within the community, the message may get lost. In this ever-changing world of information, it will take a strong voice within the community to keep the message consistently defined within the community. An organization really has to focus on allowing the individual to take ownership of the message. The individual has to stay motivated by the idea that it is possible to benefit the community, with an emphasis on how that motivation will benefit society as a whole.

7

Vision and the Community Advocate

The community advocate is the cornerstone of delivering the message of the civic honors program.

Few community organizations have the perspective to see or understand trends in civic participation. It is rare for an organization to have the perspective to look through a different lens at the community and more importantly at their position within that community. Leadership defines the vision within the community itself because it is not just a symbol of community action; it establishes the bridge for action. Having the vision to see civic participation as a necessity and providing the leadership necessary to work to develop participation can come only from a motivated leader. The university has to become an advocate for the vision of community. A graduation with civic honors program needs to be established as a central means of organizing and defining the community.

Being conscious of the level of participation within the community is necessary to understand changes that will occur. Changes in the level of participation are inevitable as individuals learn about the civic honors system. A strong community advocate with the vision to be attentive to changes in the level of participation can benefit the community. Responsibility lies in defining the path of action and providing for stewardship along that path. Being able to see the need before it exists will avert many of the potential problems within the community. This proactive stance benefits the community, enabling a focus on the bigger picture of what is possible. Having a strong advocate within the community for the civic honors program will allow its message to become a part of the community.

The idea that benefiting society is possible and that there are realistic ways of effecting change that have lasting benefits is a powerful message in and of itself. That said, the university's becoming an advocate for this message allows a national network of organizations capable of effecting change.

Understanding the position of the university within the community will have a profound effect on being able to think about the positions of organizations within the community. Organizations are working to benefit the community, and each one currently has some voice within the system. The question develops around the possibility of a university stepping into a central role within the community to provide the bridge or link, if you will, for civic honors. The abilities to facilitate the communication between organizations and to develop a comprehensive voice for the community make this a viable choice. This voice will make it easier for community leaders to spread messages about developing community and the potential of organizations to benefit society.

The university can use the civic honors program as a tool for bringing together the community. However, that tool requires the university to become an advocate for the civic honors program. Based on the assumption that the civic honors program has the capacity to motivate individuals and to benefit society as a whole, having a powerful advocate for the message promoted by a successful civic honors program will help determine the expansion of the program. Having the vision to become an advocate for the civic honors program as well as for change within the community will benefit society. That benefit will come from bringing together individuals and organizations and from educating the community about possibilities. A stronger community developed from connecting the community is the backbone of the argument for a civic honors program.

INDIVIDUALS BECOMING ADVOCATES FOR PARTICIPATION

For the individual to take ownership in participating in the community, it has to be something that the individual truly believes in.

If the individual does not believe in the ethic of community, achievement is problematic. The civic honors program is about rewarding the individual for an initial contribution of civic participation in the hopes that this civic activism outlasts the program and extends into the life of the individual. That ethic of active participation and volunteerism will promote the development of the individual as a long-term advocate for participation. Every single time an individual participates within the civic honors program, it becomes stronger.

Personal motivation to act within the community is necessary for the development of the individuals as advocates for participation within the community. If individuals cannot be motivated to work with organizations within the community, the potential for change to occur through active participation disappears. Does individual motivation matter within the community? Without the individual's motivation to participate within any program, change will never be possible. Change is developed from a large network of individuals coming together to solve the bigger problems of the community. Individuals as advocates for participation within the civic honors program have the largest potential to help develop a grass roots movement for change.

The level of participation from individuals obviously will determine the success of the civic honors program. If many individuals within the community become advocates for increasing the level of participation within the community, there is no limit to expansion of the civic honors program. A high level of civic participation among individuals strengthens the community as a whole. Having the vision that civic participation is the key to strengthening the community is necessary for the civic honors program to be successful. The power that individuals have within the community when they are empowered with a positive message of change can motivate the entire community.

PARTICIPATING ORGANIZATIONS AS ADVOCATES

The capacity for thinking about organizations as advocates involves breaking down those organizations into categories.

Thinking about the civic honors program in terms of the organizations that are willing participate in the program also helps to define the potential of the program for expansion. If organizations that participate within the civic honors program do not become advocates for the program, the benefits will not have the same advantage through the community. These organizations often have their own strong relationships with current volunteers, and without the wider scope, the participation message spreads at the organizational level. This involves thinking about the potential of faith-based organizations to reach large numbers of individuals not just in congregations and community outreach, but also by becoming a significant part of the civic honors movement. However, success will take a lot more than involving faith-based organizations. It will take athletic organizations, learning organizations, and community outreach organizations.

Developing organizations as advocates for the civic honors program allows the program to expand and adapt with changes over time. Emerging grass roots movements to address problems within the community will be able to access the civic honors program as well as well-established organizations within the community. This access will allow for a wide variety of organizations to participate in the program, fostering a strong network of civic honors collaborators within the community. The stronger the network of organizations working together to benefit the community, the more stable the civic honors program will be and the greater the potential benefits to the community.

BUILDING CONNECTIONS IN THE COMMUNITY

The long-term goal of the civic honors program is to develop a network of peo-ple within the community who are interested in their community becoming stronger than it was when they started in the program.

The idea is that not only do individuals participate within the commu-nity, but they also build connections to other people and organizations in the community. That network of people is what community is really about. As growth within the civic honors program expands, the connec-tions between individuals and organizations also increase, developing a rich set of connections within the community. Using communication as the first stepping-stone to building a larger interaction between individuals within the community will be critical to success.

The larger the network of connections within the community, the eas-ier it will become to keep individuals and organizations motivated within the community. This will provide a stable long-term benefit to the com-munity from the synergy of connections and networking, which could enable the civic honors program to expand through developing strategies. Being able to nurture connections within the community is one of the strongest ways to motivate the community through association and under-standing of the participants and the potential benefits. Organizations can use their influence together as a coalition of organizations working toward the common goal of benefiting society. Could the coalition not only uti-lize the resource consolidation the civic honors program, but also build substantial credibility for expansion of the civic honors program (Berry, 1989)?

8

Setting a Trend for the Community

Universities have the ability and a unique opportunity to take center stage in the community.

Universities can develop a set of goals for that community to identify and even set trends in community development. The university can look at the trends of active participation within the community. Using the civic honors program as a tool to gather information about developing trends also will enable using that information for motivation. Being able to understand changes in active participation can help in designing an effective program. Trends within the community not only will determine the number of individuals willing to participate over time, but also will affect the way organizations participate within the community. One may assume that the levels of participation will rise and fall within the community and that the university will be able to identify and track those trends. That assumption becomes measurable through the data collected from the civic honors program.

Being able to identify trends that cause a disconnect between individuals and organizations is necessary to identify trends within the community that are divisive. Setting a trend toward strengthening community by attempting to address the disconnect between individuals and organizations is one way to focus the vision of the community. The real question is whether an organization within the community can set a trend for the community. The university is in a unique position to spread the message of any program to a large number of people. By using this voice, which relates to the community to begin with, the university can send connect a message with the people. Having the strength to take a message and become an advocate for that message within the community requires a certain amount of commitment. For leaders within the community or university to adopt that level of commitment and spread the message of the civic honors program takes a certain kind of leader.

Strong leadership is essential to being able to set the type of example that can become a trend within the community. If a leader does not step forward to set a trend for the community, a significant gap between the community and possibility develops. The university has the natural position to step forward and be a voice for setting an agenda for the community, and part of that agenda should be setting examples for the community. Stable long-term stewardship of the important issues facing the community will be the difference between having some success and achieving what is possible. Within the civic honors program, a trend can be set for an active ethic of volunteerism. The question is whether a strong leader will emerge to deliver that message to the individuals within the community.

For an organization to take on the leadership role and begin to plan a strategic vision for the community, that organization must be an advocate for that message. Having leaders within that organization who advocate change within the community is a necessary element of delivering a strong stable civic honors program with the vision required to spread the message. Being able to start, sustain, and identify trends within the civic honors program and the community will be a difficult task. To set a leadership example without understanding the foundation for developing a motivated base within the community would be pure folly. Community leaders have to take ownership of the civic honors program and become advocates for its message, believing that it is sustainable and worthwhile.

Having the vision necessary to look at the big picture and to identify developing issues and trends requires a lot of perceptive skill. The perspective develops from looking at the community and understanding the basic motivations of individuals and organizations involved and from finding ways to leverage those motivations to bring together individuals to overcome problems within the community. Now is the time to think about what is possible and how community leaders can take advantage of the civic honors program as a tool.

TRENDS FOR INDIVIDUALS

Thinking about what is possible on the individual level is important to understanding what is achievable.

If a trend can establish successful recruiting for the civic honors program, it expands the potential for success of the program at the grass roots level. Individuals who are actively participating in the civic honors program but also are recruiting other individuals to become active participants add to the potential to expand rapidly. Looking at trends on the individual level is important to understanding how the message develops within the community. If the individual ties the power of a strong community message to an organization working to benefit the community, this message is more consistent. Developing a consistent message to benefit the community has the potential to strengthen the community as a whole.

Fostering the development of positive trends on the individual level has the potential to benefit all of society through the empowerment of individuals. The civic honors program definitely sets a trend toward involving the individual in the process of strengthening the community. Being able to identify strong individuals within the community and to educate them about how to develop the potential of recruiting into the civic honors program is a trend worth developing. The assumptions behind looking at trends at the individual level are that change can occur at the individual level and that real and lasting benefits to society will come from motivated individuals within the community. The underlying idea is that the civic honors program can enable the individual to be a major actor in developing a stronger community.

The idea behind nurturing trends at the individual level is that development of a strong grass roots movement will strengthen the civic honors program within the community. To develop that grass roots movement requires a centralized location for individuals not only to find a common message, but also to access the information necessary to participate within the community. Without information that is accessible and reliable, the individuals within the community will never be able to mobilize around one message of benefiting society. The true power of the civic honors program on the individual level comes from changing the way individuals exchange information with organizations.

TRENDS FOR ORGANIZATIONS

Organizations taking ownership in the civic honors program and becoming advocates for participation within the program and the community have the capacity to develop a strong civic honors program.

How organizations react within the civic honors program and the resulting trends will determine the course of the program. It is important to study initial reactions to learn how the civic honors program develops within the community. Trends resulting from individuals' participation with organizations will be a benchmark for the future of the civic honors program. If organizations do not become advocates for the civic honors programs, the benefits to society from the civic honors program will be limited. The university has to be attentive to the trends that develop from organizational participation. Continual attention must be paid to the direction that the organizations are taking within the civic honors program and opportunities to develop, expand, and provide leadership.

The number of organizations participating will be a strong determinant in the number of opportunities for individuals to participate in the civic honors program. If that participation is limited, the benefit to the community will not have the capacity to change the community. The assumption behind looking at trends of organizational participation is that the more organizations participate in the civic honors program, the greater the benefit to society.

TRENDS FOR COMPANIES

The message of the civic honors program is for individuals and organizations and is also meant for companies within the community.

When a prospective employer sees on a résumé that an individual has graduated with civic honors, it should say something to the employer about the individual. The résumé is reflective of that individual's commitment to the community and community service. Allowing companies to reward those individuals who have been active participants within the community in the interview process or even to reward current employees by recognizing them in the company newsletter provides external validation of such involvement.

Companies also have the ability to spread the message about the civic honors program by requiring that charities and organizations be participants in the civic honors program as a prerequisite for asking for charitable donations. Most companies are already involved in philanthropy and spend money within the community. Asking organizations to participate within the civic honors program is a way to enhance the return on investment from such philanthropy within the community. A trend of companies' acknowledging the civic honors program and discussing it within community will spread the message that the civic honors program offers.

9

Having a Positive Message

The civic honors program has to be developed while keeping a positive message about benefiting the community.

This positive message has to develop into a trend within the community that being positive about the possibilities for benefiting the community is important to actually seeing tangible benefits. If the power of the message is lost on arguments and politics, the civic honors program will not be able to define its place within the community. The basis of the civic honors movement has to be nonpartisan in nature to be able to benefit the community (Sirianni & Friedland, 2001). Having the ability to express ideas about creating a stronger community where individuals are active participants is necessary to benefit society. Addressing the disconnect between individuals and organizations needs to be handled with great leadership and stewardship. The message cannot become a negative one about how individuals do not participate within the community. It has to be about the potential for individual to be active participants.

A beginning strategy is having honest and open conversations about the ability of the community to address problems in very real ways. The civic honors program can be used to identify needs within the community and to talk about how to mobilize individuals to participate to meet those needs to benefit the community as a whole. Strong leadership within the community must focus on moving forward within the community and on the potential of accomplishment if the community becomes motivated.

10

Never Fear Collaboration

For the civic honors program to be successful and develop beyond the organizations that endeavor to build it, an effective concept for design is imperative.

During the development of a civic honors program, planners can design and redesign that program before it is implemented; thus, leaders have the opportunity to be effective designers (Clawson, 2003). Part of designing an effective civic honors program is developing the capacity for collaboration. It will not be possible to focus the community without involving as many organizations within the community as possible. Designing the program to be able to expand and work with other organizations is essential to the long-term acceptance of a civic honors program within the community.

Getting the community to work together in any way is a positive step in the right direction. Building a civic honors program designed to facilitate collaboration and focus on making connections within the community is essential to truly building a stronger community. Organizations have to adopt the mantra, "Never fear collaboration," to be successful in getting individuals to work together for the benefit of the community. Any opportunity for collaboration without extensive cost to the actors involved and without substantial risk should be encouraged. Building a stronger society through collaboration also has a secondary effect: It changes the style of leadership within the community. Civic engagement of leaders collaborating with other individuals within the community will help foster continued collaboration by building networks of trust.

THE MODEL FOR EXPANSION

Collaboration is part of the model for expansion and is essential to building a model at the national level.

Without thinking about how to motivate organizations and individuals to work together, a national model would lose a lot of the potential that a civic honors program brings to the table. The first universities to design civic honors programs will have to consider seriously and carefully record program implementation. The ultimate goal is to build implementation of the civic honors program into a model for expanding to the national level. This will require strong leadership from those universities endeavoring to design the program. Being able to think critically and evaluate every possible alternative and then being able to document those discussions into something that can be shared with other universities and organizations will require a certain level of commitment.

However, that commitment will pay dividends to the community as it becomes increasingly easy to implement a civic honors program. Someday, there will be a carefully crafted guide to the implementation of a civic honors program based on the experiences of previous programs. Such a guide would identify key trends within the civic honors movement and would explain the issues related to long-term success. Design and implantation of civic honors programs will take a lot of collaboration between universities to develop a stronger network of universities nationwide. Most significantly, colleges will be brought together under the umbrella of strengthening the community.

BUILDING FOR THE FUTURE

The future is limitless, and the potential that exists within the community is real and needs to be utilized and recognized.

One of the best ways to utilize that potential is to collaborate to facilitate change. The more thought and work put into the future of the civic honors program, the greater its potential. If universities can build a successful civic honors network, the future for expansion and collaboration will be almost self-sustaining.

If individuals and organizations within the community are not contributing to the graduation with civic honors program, long-term potential for the program is lost. The potential for working within the community is endless. With individuals and organizations as advocates for strengthening the community, it is only a matter of time before the community benefits. Having a firm belief that the community has the potential for future benefit is the basis for designing a focused strategy. If the civic honors program is not an example of thinking about what is possible in the community, its message has been lost along the way. Looking at potential as a positive and at change as essential to realizing those possibilities is the start to building for the future.

11

Thinking About Technology

In a world where things are changing faster and faster every day, it is important to embrace technology that has the potential to empower the individual.

Technology today is about bringing together people to work on a wide variety of tasks driven by business to expand the potential of communication in the workplace. Such technology has a distinct and definite ramification for the community. The community has to move forward with the technology, adapting to change at the speed of business.

Sometimes the community just thinks about business in terms of the financial contributions to the community. However, this is short sighted and is not adapting to the changes in innovation and technology. It is time for the community to think about the amount of innovation business can bring to the community in the form of expanding how people interact. Further, using that distinct background in emerging technology will help the community move forward. From the business perspective, strengthening the community helps develop a stronger labor pool and better business in general.

Community leaders must adopt the perspective to take a step back and acknowledge that they may not have a comprehensive understanding of emerging technology. It could be beneficial to utilize resources within the community to expand the ability to use technology to benefit community. This perspective will define communities that are able to move forward in a progressive way and will cast a shadow on those communities that do not utilize the capacity to connect people. Every community needs to focus on bringing together individuals; without that level of focus, accomplishing anything meaningful within the community will be impossible.

The assumption when thinking about what is possible in terms of technology is that utilizing technology can benefit the community. The assumption is that anything that can help bring together individuals is going to be beneficial to society as a whole. Relevant to the overall message of the civic honors program is the idea that developing technology makes it easier to get individuals to work together. Decreasing separation at all times is important to the community, because it means that the assumptions behind the action involve believing in the future. This is important to assist the community in integrating new technology. That integration of technology will help develop a clear path for the future; it will allow the community to build momentum at the speed of technology. Thinking in terms of the future as bringing success is always going to be a positive message.

When thinking about technology it is important to think in terms of solutions to real problems. It is possible to brainstorm a list of problems and then to determine how to apply technology to the solution. When technology applies within the problem solution framework, the power of change can be unlocked. It is important to look at every possible scenario and to think about what is possible; understanding the potential and the limitations will allow problem identification. Looking at solutions is the beginning of understanding the problems in their entirety.

The idea of using advancements in technology to help guide the community's strategy for dealing with problems is not new. Focusing on the upper bound of what is possible for the community raises the bar for expectations for achievement. It also allows individuals in the community to see a vision of the future and what can be achieved if individuals work together to accomplish something.

It is important to understand that if the community does not rally around technology and make it a cornerstone of community development, the revival of civic participation may falter. If leaders do not take control of emerging technologies, they will lose the potential to introduce them into the mainstream message of community. If only small groups and some organizations use technology, it will lose the potential for mass mobilization, and using technology in the community is really about being able to connect a large number of individuals together efficiently and effectively.

KNOWING WHAT IS POSSIBLE

Really focusing on the frontier of new technology will give a competitive edge to the community.

It is important for leaders in the community to understand not only the theory behind developing community, but also the tools that help develop community. Those tools can be modern advances in technology like those that drive the civic honors program or can be as simple as developing a platform of communication between people. The power of mailing lists and communicating through technology alleviates the cost of expensive mailing campaigns. Simple changes in adapting to the abilities of technology can have huge dividends in cost savings and in the speed of information communication.

Thinking about what it takes to speed up the flow of information is a distinct part of understanding what is possible. Right now, somewhere a research and development department is creating something that could revolutionize communication. The community need not try to become the leader in developing technology, but should become a leader in using technology to its fullest potential.

Not every technology that is developed will change the way individuals in the community work together, so it is important to attempt to identify those technologies that have the potential to "push the envelope." Every community has the resources to understand what technologies are available, because every community has individuals who work with technology. The challenge of community leaders is to identify those individuals who understand technology and to motivate them to benefit the community. Each time someone brings a unique set of experiences and insight to the table to discuss community, there is potential to strengthen the community.

Involving individuals with technical savvy empowers those individuals to make a difference in their community. This frames the discussion around what individuals can do for the community to make it stronger: the empowering idea that every individual within the community can make a difference and that the difference is meaningful and has the potential to spark innovation. Spreading the idea in the community that civic participation has potential rewards for the community and for the individual is only one of the benefits of expanding discussion on this level.

The discussion uniquely expands the possibilities for action within the community to include alternatives. This presentation of alternative courses of action expands the number of potential outcomes for the community. The community can consider various potential solutions and thus develop various strategies. Being able to assess honestly the possible community actions will broaden the desire to achieve goals and will help refine the path to achieving those goals.

Working to develop plans of action involves the development and utilization of certain technologies. Within the context of the civic honors program, the university has to identify and involve individuals within the community who can utilize technology. The university has a unique opportunity in this case because of its technology departments. With a built-in talent pool and a program that has the capacity to keep up with technology, the university can turn that talent into strength for the community.

Thus, the university can expand the potential of technology within the community and the opportunities to put that technology to use. University staff can recognize key movements in technology and use those advances to help motivate individuals within the community. However, planning and vision are necessary to implement such a program using technology. Fortunately, with strong leadership it is only a matter of time before an organization within the community steps forward and is able to see potential for strengthening the community.

THE POWER OF DATA COLLECTION

There is nothing more powerful than information management; being able to control the message and to have a complete picture about what is going on is essential to clear vision within the community.

Being able to collect data about the community is challenging but essential to understanding the long-term progress of any program. Looking at the data allows for several distinct advantages. Being able to run simulations of potential strategies and to look at developing trends allows for a more flexible perspective.

What this means for the community is that a strong, stable stewardship of issues and ideas is possible within a framework that allows a realistic assessment of what is possible as well as what is actually happening. If an organization can build networks of information accessible by the community, all organizations within the community will benefit. Centralizing the data in a way that allows individuals with the appropriate background to interpret and evaluate trends increases the capacity to utilize the data. No single organization within the community has the capacity to look at all of the data at the same time; any effort to do so would be a Herculean task. However, if all of the organizations with the community work together with the university, this task becomes manageable. Universities have the individuals with the talent to interpret and analyze data, perhaps to negate the need for a paid staff analyst within the organization.

Thus, such data can be used to help bridge the disconnect between individuals and organizations. Not being able to look at the numerical analyses of what is really going on within the community creates problems for the community because of confusing perceptions about the issues. It is much easier to address problems that are identifiable and apparent. This also allows organizations that do not have the time or resources to develop a comprehensive strategy of data analysis to allow an outside organization to bring them information on the community in a way that is unified and transparent. Being able to locate reliable information is central to refining and defining understanding of participation within the community.

BEING ACCESSIBLE

Understanding how to use technology to become more accessible is the foundation of any effort to bring people together.

The power of the Internet and Web-based communication is to bring individuals together under a common purpose to achieve things in ways that were not possible prior to this revolutionary technology. Technology can increase the efficiency of any program designed to bring people together. Often, the energy of individuals willing to participate, when met with any amount of resistance to volunteering their time, becomes diffused. Unlocking that potential energy is what being accessible is all about: bringing people together in a way that unites them in a common cause.

To achieve a significant level of Web-based communication, individuals who can design and implement the system must be involved in the process. It will take an active effort between all the individuals involved to design a system that effectively and efficiently can bring people together. The Web-based communication has to be simplistic and targeted to help individuals understand how to navigate through information and to target their efforts. This is a complex task and requires planning and maintenance of the system to adapt to changes in technology and in individual demand.

The assumption behind striving to offer accessible streams of information is that if the individual can access the information provided by the organizations, the amount of active participation from individuals will increase. Within the community, increasing the amount of active participation will be a driving force to get organizations to participate in any program to develop the community. Increasing the speed at which information travels between individuals and organizations changes the dynamic of not only accessible information, but also the quality of information available to the individual. The individual's ability to access information on demand about organizations in the community and the potential to participate really changes the way organizations recruit individuals; it allows individuals to fulfill the functions of a recruiter. They pick the organizations they want to focus on and can make choices about what they want to do and how much time they want to give to the community.

Within a system that focuses on accessibility, there remains the potential for individual disenfranchisement. Those individuals who want to participate may not be able to access easily or quickly the information they need and thus may lose focus. That possibility is a dangerous risk because it limits the amount of people willing to actively participate; for the individual, time is valuable, and the time spent looking for an organization to volunteer with is really time that could have been spent volunteering. If the community does not adapt to the speed of technology, opportunities to expand the amount of information accessible to individuals within the community will be lost.

BULLETIN BOARDS AND THE PEOPLE

One of the greatest innovations of the information technology movement has been the ability to post information to a central location where individuals who are interested and motivated can learn and interact.

The opportunity that bulletin boards present is based on the idea that discussion is best when a large number of individuals can generate ideas. Within the civic honors program, the university will benefit greatly by having an active bulletin board online that will allow free discussion of issues and ideas about the civic honors program. This bulletin board discussion will help refine ideas and allow for a potential shift in the learning curve. Individuals' thinking about ways the program could strengthen the community and actively discussing the issue allow for a tremendous amount of individual ownership. The individual is empowered by the belief that he or she is not only actively participating in the civic honors program, but also helping to develop it.

This connection between individuals and the program is a valuable tool to address and understand problems. The university can receive and react to feedback on specific issues. Focusing on issues surrounding the civic honors program without having to call an ad hoc committee or receive a report from a fact-finding commission speeds up the flow of information.

Learning about the perspectives of individuals within the program will develop understanding of how the program works and what elements of the program have the greatest power to build connections between individuals and the community.

Empowering individuals to take ownership of their own courses of action is a benefit, which is compounded by using the bulletin board system to open the door to new streams of ideas from participants. If individuals are presented with access to a system that lets them participate within the community and add a tangible benefit to society, they likely will participate in droves. Further, the level of participation will expand exponentially as the message echoes through the community. Connecting individuals with a common goal and giving them a voice to express feeling and ideas about achieving that goal provide valuable focus on the goal.

Building a connection between individuals and issues is a powerful way to get the message out about issues to individual actors within the community. For participation to be active and meaningful, individuals have to feel like they have the power to address the problems themselves and have personal ownership in the solutions. No successful program will be able to develop a successful strategy for implementation without listening to the potential participants.

Bulletin boards are just an example of how technology can bring people together; it is important to think of ways to use technology not only to refine the process, but also to connect people to the process. Thinking about the impact of technology on communication within the community is important to providing long-term stewardship of the civic honors program or any program that seeks to develop the community by addressing community needs.

FUTURE TECHNOLOGY AND EMPOWERMENT

The future path of technology will unveil a world of infinite possibility to develop the community.

If only a small amount of that potential is tapped, the possibilities for change within the community will be unprecedented. Change in the community will come in three ways: The community will become better, stronger, and faster in dealing with challenges. Being able to bridge the gap between individuals and organizations will be a fundamental change in community interaction. Stronger interaction will lead to changes in the way individuals perceive the community and how they interact with the community. The connections that develop through advances in technology will serve to strengthen existing networks and to build new ties in the community. Developing a network of trust between people who are connected, able to listen to the concerns of the community in real time, and able to react to problems as they develop will enhance the community.

Communication presents the greatest potential for bringing together individuals within the community. Organizations within the community can get their message out on issues and present a case for action that resonates with individuals who are ready to act. Community organizations will have the potential to work with the university in new ways. This project will facilitate the establishment of a well-defined network of community that is strong enough to tackle challenges in ways that will result in effective change. Change is possible, and changes in technology are inevitable within current society.

The assumptions are that change is good for the community and that technology will be a major factor driving change in the future. If technology has the potential to create change within the community and can unite the community with a well-defined positive message, the community will become stronger. Being able to empower individuals to utilize this technology to effect change will have a profound effect on society. Individuals will have a voice, powered by technology, which will echo deep into the social fabric of the community. Technology has the potential to speed up progress along the learning curve for the community and offers a path to tremendous progress and innovation. Empowering people with technology is a solution to the problem of participation; it unlocks the door to a world of community action that was harder to find before this revolutionary technology.

Individuals' having the power to come together, react to issues within the community, and learn from leaders within the community spreading a positive message about what is possible will create change in the community. The real danger exists in the community's inability to adapt to technology to allow individuals to make direct connections with each other. If the current system is rigid or stagnates, the potential based on changes in technology is lost, and individuals with the power to communicate will not do so within the forums of the community. It takes more than just leadership; it takes a progressive vision to be able to facilitate change within the community. Vision is not only necessary, it is essential to allowing change to occur in a way that will benefit the community by developing stronger ties between individuals and the community.

Fundamentally, change is possible within the community; in most respects, it is inevitable. However, the speed with which change occurs will be determined by how the community manages technology. Change will benefit society; it will develop the ability of leaders to positively impact society with programs and policies designed to facilitate communication and better understanding between all individuals within the community. Disseminating information about the possibilities of change has the potential to foster ideas that will allow social change to occur.

THE FUTURE OF E-COMMUNITY

E-community requires a new mind set for thinking about the community. Thinking about the community as moving with technology is imperative, because it is inevitable that technology will change.

Those changes in technology have the potential to drive changes in community. The two can be thought of as one continuous motion, defined by the word *e-community*. Every day it will become harder to separate the community from technology.

Within the community, change is inevitable, so why fight it? Change has to be embraced as a necessary element of strengthening the community. The assumption behind thinking about change as inevitable is that technology will change everything, and it is up to the community leadership to decide what is worth maintaining and how to manage that change. Based on this assumption, the role of a leader within the e-community is vital. Leadership is one the most important assets that a community can develop and maintain. Without strong leadership within the e-community, change will occur haphazardly. Understanding how technology will effect change within the e-community is a distinct part of understanding the path of the community.

Networks within the e-community should develop into a seamless integration of individuals and ideas. As it becomes simpler for individuals to exchange information and ideas, the e-community becomes stronger and develops a large wealth of knowledge that the community can use to develop strength. Being able to focus on change and the way it creates and addresses problem will define the success of the e-community. Without leaders focused on being long-term e-community stewards, the community will miss the opportunities that change provides.

USING FREE TECHNOLOGY RESOURCES

One of the greatest resources that the civic honors program has is developing technology. A lot of developing technology is being given away in one form or another. For instance, free server software is available, such as UNIX or Linux, which reduces the initial cost of implementing the civic honors program. If the civic honors database software develops with the same ethic and enthusiasm as these free software implementations, the possibilities for expansion are endless. Most communities already have deep and rich traditions of using free technology resources. In fact, most communities have at least one Linux user group, which is a valuable resource to find individuals who may be willing to donate some time to the civic honors program. Being able to utilize every community resource to bring together the community without having to spend copious amounts of money is always meaningful.

The power of the civic honors movement is to bring together every possible combination of individuals within the community. Focusing on bringing individuals who understand technology into the fold for the creation of a civic honors program is an important part of building a successful program. Focusing on finding emerging technologies to help bring together individuals within the community has to be a part of the civic honors program. Without that focus, the possibilities for developing a civic honors program are limited.

12

Measuring Change in the Community

The civic honors program enables determining the number of individuals trying to participate and the number of organizations looking for volunteers.

Adding this ability to look at how people are attempting to participate and how that varies over time is a very important part of the civic honors program. Demographic shifts of the region may correlate with the data collected by the civic honors program. The best indication of how to measure change in the community is how many individuals as well as organizations actively participate. Such data also can provide a useful measure of the impact of the civic honors program on the community.

Measuring change within the community is much more difficult than measuring change within the civic honors program. It will be important for organizations within the community to attempt to measure change through developing measures that can serve as indicators. One way to investigate how change occurs within the community is through surveying the community, although this would be a challenge.

The community can look at measures such as social investment, resources, production, and social capital; however, being able to look at a comprehensive set of measures within the community will deliver an accurate indication of change. It is important to be able to integrate all of these views of the community into a comprehensive model of progress.

LOOKING AT INDIVIDUAL CHANGE

The power to motivate the community comes through motivating the individuals within that community.

Measuring change within individuals is straightforward; the civic honors program internal tracking data will chart individual participation. The only follow-up required by the university is to determine the reasons why individuals are participating in the community. Determining what motivates individuals adds to the general understanding of what is going on within the community. It is easy to chart the number of individuals participating within the civic honors program. However, understanding how the civic honors program retains and motivates individuals to participate within the community will require extensive research.

Developing strategies to conduct exit surveys on the subject of what motivates individuals within the community will require strategic planning. Being able to develop accurate surveys that perhaps allow a Web-based evaluation to curb costs will help quantify benefits of this initiative. Evaluating change using emerging technology has two advantages. First, it allows the data to be generated digitally for evaluation in real time. Second, it reduces costs and automates the process, so that the smallest amount of maintenance yields the largest possible result. Focusing on the individual within the community will allow organizations to view individual change as not only necessary, but also possible.

LOOKING AT CHANGE IN THE ORGANIZATION

Organizations will become advocates for the civic honors program by believing that change can occur.

Being able to look at how organizations participate within the civic honors program will show organizations' level of commitment to strengthening the community. It also will be important to determine why organizations are participating in the civic honors program by conducting a presurvey before they post opportunities for individuals within the civic honors database. Looking at the long-term attitudes and opinions within organizations will help understand how change is occurring within the organizations in the community. Having a survey that charts those opinions every time the organization updates opportunities will allow the university to develop an accurate analysis of long-term, longitudinal trends within organizations.

Being able to analyze those long-term trends within organizations is a major stepping-stone to being able to look at change within those organizations and to identify what really makes the civic honors program work. It also will allow a statistical evaluation of how change occurs within the community. Looking at changes in organizations will be necessary to develop a big-picture evaluation of how change is occurring within the community. If the civic honors program is not changing organizational attitudes about the possibilities within the community, an opportunity to strengthen the community as a whole has been lost.

13

Potential for Expanding Around the World

Every country around the world has more in common than they do different; in fact, the basis of any society is the community.

While the models of government and the languages spoken might be different, that does not change the underlying dynamics of the community. Community development may take different routes in other nations and have distinct problems, but it is possible with the proper attention to individual cases. Any university can begin a civic honors program anywhere at any time. There always will be individuals and organizations that need better communication. The civic honors program facilitates communication within the community. The potential to expand the civic honors program is endless; eventually it may be possible to have a civic honors conference that has representatives from all nations.

The potential for expanding the civic honors program comes from the positive nature of its message. The message is definitely working on the premise that a strong community will benefit society as a whole. If the message is positive and about the benefits of a strong community, the potential is limitless for expansion. Communication is the key to spreading the message and to increasing active participation in the civic honors program. Being able to expand the message of the civic honors program to any community is part of a positive message geared at benefiting the community. Civic society does not require a pure liberal democracy. It is possible to develop programs to develop and strengthen civic society regardless of political climate (Kaviraj & Khilnani, 2001). Thus, a civic honors program can be developed, regardless of boundaries and borders. The message is powerful because it is a positive expression of the possibilities of community. Being positive without regard for geography is a major part of what makes worldwide expansion possible for the civic honors program.

BUILDING AN INTERNATIONAL COMMUNITY MODEL

It is possible to design a civic honors model that is transferable between universities.

A model has to transfer to other universities in general, creating the potential to transfer that model to universities all over the world. Universities already have partnerships and collaborations with other learning institutions all over the world. This creates the potential to use those preexisting networks to transfer the model of civic honors within that network. The same values and ethics behind the civic honors program exist in every community throughout the world. No reason exists for the civic honors program not to work in other countries.

Some small changes in the modes of communication would have to be addressed for the civic honors program to work in areas without a strong technological infrastructure, however. Communications possible through technology could be implemented using strategies conceived with long-term planning. For instance, organizations willing to participate in the civic honors program would have to standardize the volunteering opportunities. Instead of a civic honors program that is administered using Web-based technology, the program implementation would occur through publication. With the proper enthusiasm, ingenuity, and motivation, anything is possible, including effective strategies for spreading the civic honors program. The greatest potential exists when large numbers of individuals and organizations focus on the same idea and work toward expanding the potential for benefiting the community.

BRINGING TOGETHER THE INTERNATIONAL COMMUNITY

The power of the civic honors program extends beyond just benefiting the community; it gives the international community a common language and set of values and ideas to discuss.

When the international community focuses attention and motivation on implementing and spreading the message of the graduation with civic honors program, visibility creates possibility. The opportunities to share ideas benefiting the community will transcend borders and will bring together individuals and organizations around a common objective. Part of a successful implementation and expansion of the civic honors program is getting organizations used to working with each other.

Believing that working within an international framework is worthwhile and a part of bringing the international community together is part of the civic honors message. The message is that anything is possible within the community when individuals within the community are willing to work together to benefit society. Bringing the international community together as whole is one of the long-term objectives of the civic honors program. Potentially, no matter where an individual goes, the opportunities to volunteer within the community will be the same.

14

The Civic Honors Call to Action

Every individual within the community has a voice to spread the word about the civic honors program.

From talking to a neighbor to writing a letter, individuals have the power to call attention to issues within the community. The message of the civic honors program can spread through individuals within the community. The potential to engage the community increases as the message spreads. Every time an active civic honors advocate writes a letter to the media, a politician, or a university, that individual has the potential not only to inform individuals within the community, but also to send a bigger message that the community is interested in potentially beneficial ideas. Motivating the community around the idea that change is possible and that every individual within the community has the potential to help the community move in the right direction is empowering.

The civic honors program needs to have strong advocates within the community who are interested in seeing action. Being able to get the message out is part of starting any movement within the community. Having a positive message that can be spread by anyone within the community is a vibrant part of the civic honors initiative. It is more than a message, however; it is a call to action asking anyone who cares about the community to work to benefit the community. Communicating the message about the potential for benefiting the community can take on many forms, but the form that will have the largest potential benefit is having community advocates become the driving force for creating a civic honors program.

INDIVIDUAL ACTION

The driving force behind the call to action of any civic honors program or movement to benefit the community is getting individuals involved.

Being able to facilitate individual action within the community is the first step to building a civic honors program. Individuals have to be the ones to advocate creating a civic honors program, because individuals will be the backbone of the program. The day individuals who advocated the creation of a civic honors program have the potential to become volunteers within the community, the civic honors dream becomes a reality. Then, individuals can sit back and think about what action they can take not only to generate support for a civic honors program, but also to benefit the community in general.

That is a powerful shift in thinking about community: looking at the potential instead of at what needs work. Potential for individual action becomes the motivation for working within the community. A civic honors program has the potential to be a part of the community, backed by strong support from individuals. To realize that potential will take hard work and dedication from individuals. Individual action is necessary for not only implementing a civic honors program, but also creating and sustaining the message. Active individual participation is part of building a stronger community and a cornerstone of developing a civic honors program.

ORGANIZATIONAL ACTION

When organizations begin to take action within the community and spread the message about the civic honors program with current volunteers, staff, and families, it will drive the message.

If organizations do not become advocates for the civic honors program, it will be difficult to increase participation and expand the civic honors program. At the heart of the civic honors program is organizational participation. The civic honors program is not about finding volunteers for organizations; however, that is a side effect of wanting to increase participation within the community. Organizations will benefit from active participation of individuals within society, just as individuals will benefit from organizations' being active and vibrant within the community. As organizations increasingly become advocates for the civic honors program, the potential for expansion grows with each new action to benefit the community.

Organizational actions to benefit the community will define the civic honors movement as striving to tap the potential of the community. Being able to take action within the community is an opportunity that should resonate with organizations that are working to benefit the community. Enhancing the potential for benefiting the community in any way should be the goal of any organizations working in the community. Generating action from such organizations is only the first step to cultivating the message of civic honors.

THE POWER OF THE MEDIA

The media is a part of the community with the potential to bring issues to the forefront of the public mind.

Individuals within the media have the potential to bring issues in front of the community by developing a message that resonates, with a potential ripple effect from sharing ideas with so many individuals within the community. If the civic honors message resonates through the media, the media have the power to spread the word about the program. The media can raise a collective call for action within the community. Each story about the potential or actions of the civic honors program creates the catalyst that one new individual will learn about civic honors.

Individuals can advocate a positive message within the community. The potential of the civic honors program to become a reality grows exponentially with every story. Not only do active participants in the civic honors program feel that what they are doing is really benefiting the community, but their actions also serve as a clear message to others. Because the college is part of the community and supported by the community, through tax dollars or perhaps gifts to the foundation, the college is viewed as a partner in community by giving something back to the community. That potential is the real power of the media for uniting individuals and organizations behind the message that strengthening the community is possible. Reporting that positive change is not only occurring but also that positive social change strengthens the social fabric. This brand of civic journalism, in a positive use of the power of the media, can energize a community behind a story that is positive about the community.

References

Alinsky, S. D. (1971). *Rules for radicals: A practical primer for realistic radicals*. New York: Random House.

Barber, B. R. (1984). *Strong democracy: Participatory politics for a new age*. Berkeley: University of California Press.

Barnard, C. I. (1938). *The functions of the executive*. Cambridge, MA: Harvard University Press.

Bell, M. (1999). Volunteering: Underpinning social action in the civil society for the new millennium. In M. Akuhata-Brown (Ed.), *Civil society at the millennium*. West Hartford, CT: Kumarian Press.

Bermeo, N. G., & Nord, P. G. (2000). *Civil society before democracy: Lessons from nineteenth-century Europe*. Lanham, MD: Rowman & Littlefield.

Berry, J. M. (1989). *The interest group society* (2nd ed.). Glenview, IL: Scott, Foreman.

Blumethal, M. (1979, January 29). Candid reflections of a businessman in Washington. *Fortune Magazine, 36-49*.

Bozeman, B., & Straussman, J. D. (1990). *Public management strategies: Guidelines for managerial effectiveness*. San Francisco: Jossey-Bass.

Carlsen, C. J., Lindahl, N., & Lindahl, S. (2004). Civic honors program at Johnson County Community College. *Journal for Civic Commitment, 4*, 1-9.

Clawson, J. G. (2003). *Level three leadership: Getting below the surface* (2nd ed.). Upper Saddle River, NJ: Prentice Hall.

Covey, S. R. (1989). The 7 habits of highly effective people. New York: Simon & Schuster.

Dionne, E. J. (1998). *Community works: The revival of civil society in America*. Washington, DC: Brookings Institution Press.

Downs, A. (1966). *Bureaucratic structure and decision making*. Santa Monica, CA: Rand.

Fukuyama, F. (1995). *Trust: Social virtues and the creation of prosperity*. New York: Free Press.

Goodnow, F. J. (1967). *Politics and administration: A study in government*. New York: Russell & Russell.

Gulick, L. H., & Urwick, L. F. (1937). *Papers on the science of administration*. New York: Columbia University, Institute of Public Administration.

Johnson, S. (1998). *Who moved my cheese?* New York: Simon & Schuster.

Katz, D., & Kahn, R. L. (1966). *The social psychology of organizations*. New York: Wiley.

Kaviraj, S., & Khilnani, S. (2001). *Civil society: History and possibilities*. Cambridge, UK; New York: Cambridge University Press.

Lipsky, M. (1980). *Street-level bureaucracy: Dilemmas of the individual in public services*. New York: Russell Sage Foundation.

Margalit, A. (1996). *The decent society*. Cambridge, MA: Harvard University Press.

Meier, K. J. (1979). *Politics and the bureaucracy: Policymaking in the fourth branch of government*. North Scituate, MA: Duxbury Press.

Merton, R. K. (1957). *Social theory and social structure* (Rev. and enl. ed.). Glencoe, IL: Free Press.

Mintzberg, H. (1979). *The structuring of organizations: A synthesis of the research.* Englewood Cliffs, NJ: Prentice-Hall.

Osborne, D., & Gaebler, T. (1992). *Reinventing government: How the entrepreneurial spirit is transforming the public sector.* Reading, MA: Addison-Wesley.

Putnam, R. D. (2000). *Bowling alone: The collapse and revival of American community.* New York: Simon & Schuster.

Putnam, R. D. (2002). *Democracies in flux: The evolution of social capital in contemporary society.* Oxford, UK; New York: Oxford University Press.

Rouner, L. S. (2000). *Civility.* Notre Dame, IN: University of Notre Dame Press.

Rourke, F. E. (1984). *Bureaucracy, politics, and public policy* (3rd ed.). New York: HarperCollins.

Simon, H. A. (1947). *Administration behavior: A study of decision-making processes in administrative organization.* New York: Macmillan.

Sirianni, C., & Friedland, L. (2001). *Civic innovation in America: Community empowerment, public policy, and the movement for civic renewal.* Berkeley: University of California Press.

Skocpol, T., & Fiorina, M. P. (1999). *Civic engagement in American democracy.* Washington, DC; New York: Brookings Institution Press, Russell Sage Foundation.

Stanton, K. (1999). Promoting civil society: Reflections on concepts and practice. In M. G. Schechter (Ed.), *The revival of civil society: Global and comparative perspectives.* New York: St. Martin's Press.

Taylor, F. W. (1911). *The principles of scientific management.* New York: Harper & Brothers.

Thompson, J. D. (1967). *Organizations in action: Social science bases of administrative theory*. New York: McGraw-Hill.

Willoughby, W. F. (1918). *The movement for budgetary reform in the states, by William Franklin Willoughby*. New York, London: D. Appleton.

Wilson, W. (1889). *The state: Elements of historical and practical politics. A sketch of institutional history and administration*. Boston: D. C. Heath.

Wolfe, A. (1989). *Whose keeper? Social science and moral obligation*. Berkeley: University of California Press.

Index

978-0-595-38979-7
0-595-38979-1